As The Twig Is Bent

Kenneth Jernigan
Editor

Large Print Edition

A KERNEL BOOK
published by
NATIONAL FEDERATION OF THE BLIND

Table of Contents

Kenneth Jernigan, Executive Director
National Federation of the Blind

EDITOR'S INTRODUCTION

by Kenneth Jernigan

There is a well known saying that as the twig is bent, so grows the tree.

What is true of plants is also true of people. The poet Wordsworth said, "The child is father of the man." He meant, of course, that our behavior and beliefs as adults are, to a large extent, determined by what happens to us when we are growing up.

This third Kernel Book is largely focused on that theme—what today's blind children are being taught about themselves and what happened to yesterday's blind children, those who are today's adults. As we of the National Federation of the Blind have so often said, the real problem of blindness is not the blindness itself but the mistaken notions and misunderstandings about blindness which are so widely prevalent in society. The first two Kernel Books (*What Color is the Sun* and *The Freedom Bell*) also dealt with this theme, but the present volume has a particular emphasis on blind children and what lies ahead for them. Every day all of us are, at least to some degree, bending the twig that will determine the final shape of their lives.

In this book I have tried to acquaint you with quite a number of blind children and adults, and I have tried to do it at something more than merely the surface level. These are people I know—friends, former students, and colleagues. I think they are people that you, too, will want to know. In the process I hope you will gain an increased understanding of what blind people are like. Mostly we're just like you. We cry if we have reason to—but not because of blindness. And we laugh if something's funny—but, again, not because of blindness. Our lives are as varied, as interesting, or as dull as yours. It all depends on how the twig is bent, how the tree grows, and what opportunities and environment we have.

I don't know how many more Kernel Books we will print, but if this one gets the warm reaction which the first two have received, there will probably be others. Meanwhile the present volume is now being widely distributed, hopefully to do its bit to help improve the climate of public opinion about blindness. Every day we bend the twig.

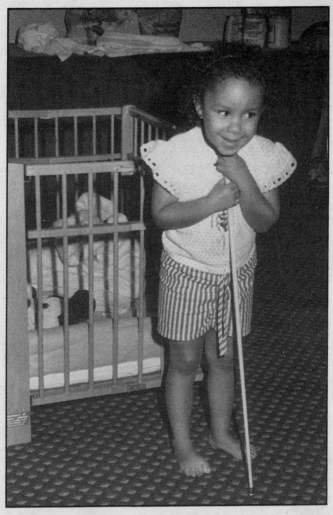

Emily Robinson. It's her future we are talking about.

WHY LARGE TYPE

The type size used in this book is 14 Point for two important reasons: One, because typesetting of 14 Point or larger complies with federal standards for the printing of materials for visually impaired readers, and we wanted to show you exactly what type size is necessary for people with limited sight.

The second reason is because many of our friends and supporters have asked us to print our paperback books in 14 Point type so they too can easily read them. Many people with limited sight do not use Braille. We hope that by printing this book in a larger type than customary, many more people will be able to enjoy these heartwarming and inspirational stories.

In the '60s Kenneth Jernigan walks through a parking lot in Des Moines, Iowa.

TO PARK OR NOT TO PARK

by Kenneth Jernigan

As those who have read previous Kernel books know, I have been blind since birth and grew up on a farm in Tennessee. After attending the state school for the blind and going to college for undergraduate and graduate degrees, I returned to the Tennessee School for the Blind for four years as a teacher, hoping not only to teach something useful to blind youngsters but also (if I could) to serve as a role model and a stimulus to accomplishment.

Then, from 1953 to 1958 I taught at California's training center for blind adults—again, trying to act as a role model and provide stimulation and encouragement. In fact, my primary task was to help those who came to the Center to examine blindness and their attitudes about it; to understand that they could still be competitive, productive members of society; and that they could not have the privileges of full citizenship without also assuming its responsibilities.

In 1958 I went to Iowa to become Director of the State Commission for the Blind, which administered a training center and other programs. Once more, I found myself examining with my trainees and students what blindness was really like, not just what it was thought to be like. How many special privileges should we take—or, for that matter, even want? What did we owe to society, and what to ourselves? How important was it to avoid offending well-intentioned sighted people who offered help that we felt we didn't need and what long-term effect would our actions have upon us and other blind people, as well as upon the members of the sighted public? Such discussions led to difficult soul searching—especially as we related them to our daily behavior. Of course, I was not just dealing with what my students felt and did but also with my own attitudes and conduct. Self deception is one of the easiest and most dangerous mistakes that a person can make.

As Director of the Iowa State Commission for the Blind, I frequently had business at the State Capitol. Ordinarily there was no trouble finding a parking place quite close to the building. However, from January until some time in the late spring or early summer the legislature was in session, and the Capitol was always crowded. Correspondingly, the Capitol grounds and parking areas were filled with cars, and if one arrived after 7:30 in the morning, he or she was likely to have to walk several blocks. If one is not in a hurry and the weather is pleasant (as, for instance, in early May with the birds singing, the sun

shining, and the appropriations settled), such walking may be good for
both body and soul, evoking thoughts
of a just providence and a well-ordered
world; but if the time is January and
the snow lies deep on the ground (with
legislators to meet and appropriations
to justify), the perspective changes.

Now, it so happens that in the Iowa
of that day I was a public figure of
considerable note, treated with respect
and deference. Therefore, when I trav-
eled by automobile to the Capitol to
transact this or that piece of business,
the security guards were pleased to
see me and offer assistance. There was
at the very door of the Capitol a parking place reserved for the handicapped, and I was a blind person. The
security guards insisted that I take
the parking place. More than that:
They were hurt and offended if I
indicated that I would park elsewhere
and walk back in the snow like everybody else.

The problem was not the guards or my colleagues in government or the general public. All would have been glad to have me use the handicapped parking place. No, that is an understatement. They would have felt downright good about it.

The problem was not with them. It was with me. I knew that I could walk as well as anybody else and that (regardless of technicalities or public misconceptions) the intent which had led to the enactment of the handicapped parking permit law was to provide easy access to the building for those who had trouble in walking and truly needed it. Yet, I like comfort and approval as well as the next person. It was not pleasant to walk through the cold, wet Iowa snow in January, and it was not satisfying to hear the tone of disappointment and hurt in the voices of the security guards when I declined the use of the space, regardless of how courteously and appreciatively I did it. And it was not a matter which could be faced, settled once and for all, and then put behind me. It happened over and over—because, as I have already said, I had frequent business at the State Capitol in January, and the snow storms came with discouraging regularity. So my Federationism and my bodily comfort, my wish to be honest and consistent and my wish to be polite and thought of as a good fellow—in short, my spiritual aspirations and my bodily desires—were in continuous conflict.

What do you think I did? In the circumstances what would you have done? Whoever says that the world is not filled with temptations (for the blind as well as for the sighted) is either a naive nincompoop or a barefaced liar. Of such is humanity made—neither angel nor devil but somewhere between, and always becoming.

WHAT LYNDEN HAS TO HEAR

by Lauren L. Eckery

In What Color is the Sun *and* The Freedom Bell, *the first two Kernel Books, I introduced Laurie Eckery and her daughter Lynden. Laurie is blind and Lynden is sighted. Because of Laurie's moving articles, Lynden has become quite well known to the members of the National Federation of the Blind throughout the country. We have watched her and her mother face and deal with the problems that confront a blind mother as she struggles to keep her sighted child from absorbing the mistaken notions about blindness that abound in a well-meaning but uninformed society. Lynden is a well-adjusted, normal child with healthy attitudes—but it has not been easy. Here is Laurie's account of some of what has happened.*

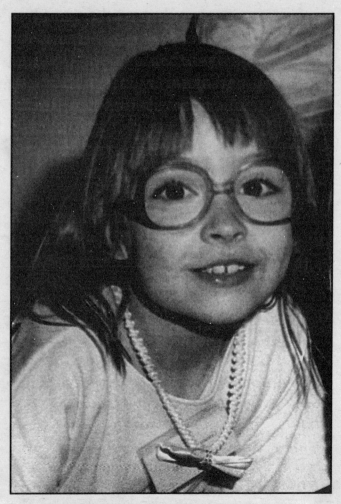

Lynden Eckery.

It is said that babies know when they're hungry, that they know when they need to eat and what they should eat. I believe it is also true that babies know whom to trust and whom to respect. It also appears that they have, at a very early age, a very good grasp of common sense.

When I first entered Lynden into Blossom Time Child Care, I had questions in my mind: How are those kids going to see my blindness? What will be the effect on Lynden?

Some child psychologists tell us that children start out quickly learning what's best for them and seeking it and then get confused when adults' values, standards, and attitudes are forced upon them.

Several weeks ago I had joined Lynden's group for lunch, as I always do after our music lesson. Most of the children had finished eating, but two girls in the opposite corner from me had the most interesting discussion:

Anne: "Her plate's almost empty, but how can she eat it?"

Beth: "Well, you saw, didn't you? She found it with her fork and ate it, so she can do it."

Anne: "I don't understand; like this morning Lynden didn't bring her in to eat. How did she get here?"

Beth: (with some disgust): "Well, Anne, you saw her walk in here. I saw you watching her. She hit the table with her cane, touched her chair, and sat down. So, she did it."

Anne: "But—but how can she do it if she can't see? Oh, yeah, she did it, so she can do it!"

How often do adults see exactly what we do and hear exactly what we say and still not believe it? How flimsy is "seeing is believing."

A few days ago I was in the hallway helping Lynden put on her coat. A mother and a small child were about to leave.

Mother (in hushed voice, of course): "No, let's wait. I want to see if she needs help."

Child: "Mom! Let's go! She doesn't need help."

Mother: "Okay, but I just want to make sure."

Child: "Mom, she does it all the time. She walks Lynden over here and home and helps her with her coat all the time."

I didn't say a word. With coat properly zipped, snapped, and hood tied, Lynden and I walked past them and left.

I couldn't help but think about these children's instructive conversations when the other day Lynden and I were approaching a cab on our way to preschool. As the driver opened the door and Lynden climbed in in her usual energetic manner, the driver admonished: "Hold on little lady. Aren't you going to help your mommy into the cab first?"

Lynden, knowing how unnecessary that was, continued onto her side of the seat. I wondered how shocked the driver was as I stepped up rather than down into the cab, sat my bottom onto the seat rather than the floor of the cab, and even proceeded to shut the door rather than open it.

I had little time to wonder, for the driver's next question, before even inquiring about our destination, was (addressed to Lynden, of course): "I bet you take real good care of your mommy all of the time, don't you sweetie?" Though Lynden didn't comment, I'm sure she heard it.

Another time, when the weather was a little warmer, we were walking to preschool. We were standing at 50th and Chicago Streets in Omaha, where there is a school crossing light. As we approached, I noticed that there was a child patrol ready to punch the light.

Several other children were hanging about, waiting for the light to change. Suddenly a mother of one of the children came up behind me and said to the children: "Don't worry, I'll take care of her."

Knowing what she meant, I thought to myself, "Oh no you won't." As the light changed, I took a larger stride than usual, which caused Lynden to run, and we were off just in time to escape the mother's hand on the back of my coat. Again, Lynden did not respond, but I know she heard.

One of these days, she's going to respond, and I wonder what her response will be. Will she agree with the adults around us that we are incompetent, or will she see us as we are? I ask this not only of Lynden but of children of blind parents everywhere.

Barbara Pierce goes where she likes with independence and ease.

HOW DIFFERENT IT MIGHT HAVE BEEN

by Barbara Pierce

Barbara Pierce was a teenager in the fifties. There was no Parents of Blind Children Division of the National Federation of the Blind then. Parents did the best they could, but most of what they did they had to do alone. Without help it was hard to escape prevailing negative attitudes, and sometimes (even with the best intentions) terrible mistakes were made. Here, with sensitivity and love, Barbara Pierce shares with us the intimate details of one such mistake her parents made.

When I was small, it was very important to my mother that I look at the people with whom I was speaking, whether or not I could actually see them. She also insisted that I be neatly and appropriately dressed. As I grew up, paging through *Seventeen* did not interest me at all since I could not see the pictures, but she taught me to care about fashion, color, and style as well as the importance of making as good a visual impression as possible. All these values my mother communicated to me in a thousand little ways. She did not indulge in long lectures, though I got my share of sermonettes after lapses in my behavior or my dress, and for these and the life-long impact they had on me I am extremely grateful.

But I also remember what happened when my father announced to me that I was to begin learning to use the long white cane. I was sixteen, and my sight had been so poor for a number of years that I had never begun the normal process of going places by myself. My first reaction was keen anticipation. My friends were getting their drivers' licenses; I was being given something roughly equivalent, though more precious because it was so personal and so long-delayed. I yearned for the independence that is the birthright of us all. Like all teenagers, I wanted freedom, but until now that impulse had been stifled by my inability to move around confidently on my own. I could hardly wait to begin my lessons, but there was a two-week delay. And during those fourteen days the damage was done.

It was no one's fault. My parents had had no contact with competent blind adults. There was no Parents of Blind Children Division; in fact, they hadn't even heard about the National Federation of the Blind. All they understood was that blind beggars carried white canes. They had seen pathetic blind people creeping along the streets of Pittsburgh, randomly poking their white canes at objects and other people. They must have been appalled at the prospect of their bright, well-adjusted daughter being reduced to such a means of mobility.

I don't remember that they said a word about these impressions to me. My father did warn me that my mother was upset about the cane, and he suggested that I keep it out of sight as much as possible. I began to realize that there was to be no excited chatter about what I was learning and where I was going. I would not be given errands to run for my mother. We were to pretend that the cane did not exist. I would use it only when there was no other option, and in my loving family, there was always another option.

By the time I met my travel teacher, I was frightened of the ordeal ahead and repelled by the idea of the white cane. He was going to make me travel places alone. People were going to stare at me. Students who did not realize that I was blind would know the truth. If I could have swallowed that cane, I would have done so.

I became an expert at getting rid of it. As soon as I got to school on the days when I was to have a travel lesson, I would get permission to go early to my locker to dump it—I certainly would not have been seen dead carrying it on other days. When I returned from school at the end of travel lesson days, I slid the cane quickly down along the wall beside the front door where it lay concealed behind the curtains until I could spirit it off to my room later. On days when my lesson kept me tied up on expeditions after school, I agonized because I knew that my mother was at home worrying about what might be happening to me. There was no triumph in these small victories over dependence; they were paid for by my mother's anguish. And the cost seemed to me entirely too high.

On balance, however, I was very lucky. The travel instruction I received was very good, and even though after

I finished my three months of lessons I did not use it again until I went to college, I managed to remember what I had been taught. Above all I am lucky because twelve years later I found the National Federation of the Blind. There, for the first time, I met healthy attitudes about blindness, Braille, and the white cane. Though delayed, I finally found again the satisfaction in independence that had been snuffed out fourteen years before.

Now that I am a parent I know with painful clarity that all of us make mistakes in raising our children. For the most part my parents did it right. They were determined that I should have every chance they could give me to succeed in life. Their instincts were largely sound and their attitudes healthy. But how different it might have been if only they had known the National Federation of the Blind.

HOW DIFFERENT IT IS

by Carol Castellano

I urge you to think carefully about the story you are about to read and to compare it to the one you have just read—"How Different it Might Have Been," by Barbara Pierce. Today, there is a Parents Division of the National Federation of the Blind and Serena Castellano's life is forever changed because of its existence and her parents' participation in it. I've named Serena's story "How Different It Is," and I think you will see why.

Last Christmas, when she was five years old, our daughter Serena received a cane from Santa Claus. To be sure, her father and I were a lot more excited about it than she was that first day, but it wasn't long before Serena discovered just what it would mean to have a cane in her life.

Queen Serena and brother Superman at Halloween.

She realized immediately that by holding that long object out in front of her, she could avoid bumping into things with her nose. She also found that she could get advance warning of steps, curbs, changes in the terrain, and the like. She no longer had to rely on holding someone's hand to avoid potential danger. Suddenly she was free!

It took her about a week and a half to incorporate the new tool into her existing repertoire of travel skills— and then there was no stopping her. The sidewalk was hers. Unfamiliar stairways—no problem. The way to our neighbors' house was easily learned and Serena strolled over to deliver a package. At the mall she was free to explore corridors and enjoy the echoes. Finding elevator doors was a snap; escalators provided great amusement (for her, not me). We were able to begin teaching her how to cross our quiet street alone. We began to walk to the park like other families, holding hands sometimes for the pure pleasure of it and not because we had to.

One day my husband and I walked over with the children to the local school to vote. While we were busy signing in, Serena went off exploring. She followed the strains of an orchestra which was rehearsing in the school auditorium, a few hallways away. Halfway down the aisle, heading for the stage, was the new Miss Independence. What possibilities the cane opened up!

I recall how it used to strike me as a little odd to see in the National Federation of the Blind's magazine, the *Braille Monitor*, picture after picture of people posing with their canes. Were they showing pride in being blind, I wondered? Were they trying to prove a point? Eventually I came to understand that the white cane is both a symbol of independence for blind people and a basic tool of making independence a reality. Matter-of-factly showing the cane in a photograph expresses the fundamental normalcy of blind people's lives.

In this year's Halloween picture of my children, the Queen of the Prom stands holding her cane next to brother Superman. It's not a display; it's not a soapbox issue. To us, a cane in Serena's hand is just the most normal thing. When our NFB friends gathered for a picnic in our backyard, Serena at one point was hanging around in the kitchen comparing canes with the rest of the gang. Just the most natural thing.

When I look back, I realize that getting the cane was the most significant event to happen to our family this year. It vastly changed Serena's level of independence; it changed mine.

At Grandma's house, we can simply direct her to the steps; no longer do I have to hang onto her along with anything else I might be carrying; she can proceed independently at her own pace. At the library I can rush ahead with my pile of books, without worrying about her tripping on the steps or falling into the fountain. When we arrive at friends' houses, she can navigate the front walks and stairways herself. Serena goes from our car in the driveway, along the walk, up the front steps, and into the house alone; I do not have to walk her. Since we are in and out of the car so many times each day, this skill was very important to my freedom.

The cane greatly raised our expectations. It is natural now for Serena to move along independently. We expect this of her; more importantly, she expects it of herself. Would Serena have progressed as much if she hadn't had a cane? I think not. Her curiosity and urge to explore would have been thwarted; she would not have been able to move about nearly as freely beyond the four walls of our home. Her development would have been needlessly hampered.

It is hard to believe that canes are not given as a matter of course to young blind children, since the cane is probably the most important external factor in the development of independence.

It is impossible to understand—and chilling to ponder—why anyone would argue against normal, natural independence in a child's life. That is what the cane makes possible. It provides the opportunity for the blind child to make the normal moves away from his or her parents, to be just like any other child, expected and encouraged to venture with increasing independence into the world.

One day a few weeks ago, Serena's cane got stuck in a crack, and when she pulled it out it broke. The magnitude of the disaster suddenly struck her.

"Ooooh," she whined, "now we're going to have to hold hands."

DO YOU WANNA GO TO THE STORE, TED?

by Ted Young

Only rarely in life is one's fate determined by a single irreversible act. Most of the time we look back and notice that a series of small events and decisions have shaped our outlook on life and our skills for meeting its challenges.

Ted Young is the president of the National Federation of the Blind of Pennsylvania. Here he writes about such a small but important episode in his own life. All parents of blind children should take heart from the courage shown by Ted's mother. Here is the story:

The other day I had occasion to wonder why it is that some blind persons are more willing to be independent than others. Yes, I know that this is true of sighted people as well, but that truism was not the point of my contemplation. Anyway, the question carried me back in thought to my first real assertion of independence. I don't know its relevance for anyone else, but perhaps it would prove helpful to a parent confronted with a similar situation.

My parents were not particularly over-protective. My father figured out that I could tell if a fish was biting by holding the line and taught me how to fish. My mother talks about how hard it was to follow the advice of the first expert in blindness she ever talked to by letting me wander about the house, bumping into things on my own. But, hard or not, she sat back and let me do it. The problem was that my parents were no more prepared than others to deal with a blind child, and there wasn't a lot of professional help or advice available in central Pennsylvania. As a result, although they knew what I could do when I was being watched or was on familiar territory, they had their fears about letting me be outside the house by myself.

How well I remember that familiar, friendly house of my childhood. Despite the leaking roof and the landlord's complaining because the rent was overdue, despite the many times my mother had little to put on the table for a meal, it was security and home. My world was my often-grouchy father, my always-caring and loving mother, and my three sometimes-okay sisters. I vividly remember being pulled from that security at the age of four to be dropped into the unfamiliar environs of the Overbrook School for the Blind, where I would spend nine months a year until high school graduation.

As time went by I learned to wander, play, and enjoy things independently on the grounds of Overbrook. Here there was no question. I was out on the sidewalks and grounds playing, running, or walking independently with my friends. I was, in short, experiencing my own capacities.

Now we come to that sultry summer day the recollection of which started these ruminations. I can't remember whether I was seven or eight, but I know that I had been to Charlie's, the nearby grocery store, many times with my sisters. What a great place it was—filled with the pleasant smells of meats, vegetables, coffee and run by a friendly owner who gave candy to the kids. To get there one needed only to walk down the front steps of my house, make a left turn, walk a half block to the corner, turn left again, and walk another half block. That's right: no alleys or streets to cross, no big deal, unless you happen to be the caring mother who doesn't know what best to do for her blind child.

I'm not sure when it occurred to me that, although my sisters were sent to the store all the time, my mother never asked me to go. I do know that on the day in question none of my sisters could be found, and my mother was complaining that she would have to drop what she was doing and go to the store herself. I told her not to worry; I would go for her. That offer was immediately and firmly declined. Although I cannot remember the argument that followed, I do remember telling my mother that I could do it, and I remember her stating that I wasn't going to try. I ended the argument by telling her that I was going to the store, and she could find me there. She replied that I'd better not. I guess she didn't believe me because she eventually went upstairs, at which point I sneaked out the door and was on my own. Down the street and around the corner to Charlie's I went, feeling guilty but good. The problem was that once I got to Charlie's, I had no money to spend, and I needed to wait there since I wanted my mother to come and see that I could make it on my own. I did the only thing I could think of at the time, which was to sit on the front step of the store and play with a leaf.

I won't go into the beating I got for disobedience or the day or two that followed in which I practiced nonverbal resistance. I was furious to realize that my demonstrated abilities were being ignored and discounted and was determined not to give in. The only protest I could think to make was silence. Although I never discussed it with her, I believe that my mother was torn between the need to punish disobedience and her recognition of my need to be treated like any other child. That was the situation two days later when my mother helped with a major step in my development by phrasing the simple question, "Do you wanna go to the store, Ted?"

Catherine Horn Randall takes the oath of office as city alderman in Jacksonville, Illinois.

PARTIALLY SIGHTED, REALLY BLIND

by Catherine Horn Randall

Catherine Horn Randall is First Vice President of the National Federation of the Blind of Illinois and an Alderman serving in the Jacksonville, Illinois, City Council.

One rainy afternoon a young mother stood across the street from Main Hall on the MacMurry College campus in Jacksonville, Illinois, watching the busy, laughing college co-eds come and go. She cried for her four-year-old daughter who might not have the opportunity to go to college or to lead a full life, because she only had partial sight in her right eye. She was afraid and wondered about Cathy's future, and all she knew to do was to have Cathy evaluated by the professional staff of the Illinois Braille

and Sight Saving School in Jacksonville.

The professionals told her that
Cathy had so much sight that she
wouldn't need to bother with Braille.
The bewildered young parents were
grateful to the experts for their advice;
who else could they turn to? The
school didn't tell them that the National Federation of the Blind even existed. Cathy's parents took her home,
determined to enroll her in the sight
saving program in Quincy, Illinois.

From this point on, I shall tell my
own story. As I look back at the enor-
mous implications to my life and to my
education from being denied the opportunity to learn Braille as a child, I
am as angry and frustrated now as my
mother was afraid for my future in
1951.

I happen to be an only child, and I
like to think that I was constructively
spoiled by my parents. They could not
have been more supportive of me. If

they had received common-sense guidance, I know I would have learned Braille. Whatever I needed to help with my education, my parents enthusiastically provided. If we had only known it, what we needed most was the National Federation of the Blind, Braille, and cane travel skills. Unfortunately for me, we used the term "partially sighted" while I was growing up. I wasn't really blind, because I had some sight. So I didn't think of myself as blind until I began losing my remaining vision in my late twenties.

I was a blind child and a blind college student who was trying to get along without either of the most important skills of blindness, namely Braille and cane travel.

I took typing lessons when I was ten, and again in both junior and senior high. Typing, I believe, is another essential skill for blind and legally blind students.

A partially blind student who reads print and takes notes with flair pens or markers and uses tapes is still greatly handicapped if he or she does not know Braille. I didn't have much confidence in myself in high school or college, and I think not having the skills of blindness was part of the reason although I did not realize it at the time.

Eye strain was a constant problem for me in school. How wonderful and practical it would have been to make an easy transition from print work to Braille when I used my eyes too much.

For years my father tutored me every night in math. My mother read to me so much that by my senior year in high school she had damaged her vocal chords. I always loved school despite the hard work. I was feature editor for both my junior and senior high newspapers.

I earned a bachelor of arts degree from that same MacMurry College, where my mother had despaired for my future nineteen years earlier. College took me four and a half years and four straight summers to complete. I am now convinced that, if I had had good Braille skills, I would have been able to handle four courses a semester like everyone else instead of taking only three. I had a totally blind friend a year behind me in college who took full course loads each semester and used Braille.

To blind and partially blind students I would say this—and I would say it with every fiber of my being: Join and become active in the National Federation of the Blind. It is the greatest gift you can ever give yourself. Take the initiative to learn Braille and cane travel. This may seem a tall order, but believe me, it is an essential one. You will find the role models that you always needed in the National Federation of the Blind. You will learn that it is respectable to be blind.

ADVICE FROM A SEVEN-YEAR-OLD

by Tim Day

Tim is 7 years old and attends Roosevelt Elementary School in Bellingham, Washington, where he is in the first grade. Tim sent this to me in Braille. As you can see, he has some advice for parents of blind children.

Tim's mother, Debbie Day, is an active and enthusiastic member of the National Federation of the Blind and its Northwest Parents Division. She also co-ordinates the Blindness and Adoption Network of the national NFB Parents of Blind Children Division.

Blind children don't see. They must use a cane. Canes help a lot. Blind children must know what things are. Some blind children haven't been to a rectory. Some blind children haven't been in a taxi. Others haven't

Tim Day doesn't have to worry about the light or getting into an awkward position when he reads in bed. He simply lies comfortably with the Braille book beside him.

been in a motor home. Go see things with your children.

Blind children read Braille. They must have Braille books. Braille is fun! I like to read and write Braille. I have an electric Braille writer. It has one-handed extension keys because I have cerebral palsy and my left hand is not strong. I have a Braille Speak and Spell and have learned how to spell lots of new words. I like to get a perfect score.

A MATTER OF ATTITUDE

by Seville Allen

Thoughtful readers of Kernel books will recognize a recurring theme—that many of the problems of blindness are not caused by blindness itself but by attitudes about it. Sometimes the attitudes causing the problem are held by sighted people about the blind. But very often the problem attitudes are held by blind people about themselves. Here Seville Allen relates an unusual and ironic incident which makes the point.

I recently moved into a neighborhood that is convenient for walking to shopping and community activities. Since a short walk will get a person most anywhere, many other blind people live in the area. On two different occasions, while waiting for a traffic light to change, a blind man asked me if I would help him across the street. Both times I said that I would.

In the first incident the man placed his hand on my shoulder, the light changed, and we crossed the street. The man thanked me and continued walking down the sidewalk.

The second time the man asked for assistance the story remained the same until we reached the opposite side of the street. My cane clicked on a pole. The man asked what the noise was. I told him that it was my cane hitting the light pole.

The man asked, "Cane?" I said yes, that I am also blind. His trust turned to immediate anger. I was informed in a loud voice that I was terribly inconsiderate to have endangered both of our lives.

I share this story because it points out how our attitude about blindness can cause us to limit ourselves and/or our belief about ourselves. In this case we were safely across the street, but rather than think about that, the man acted on his apparent belief that it is dangerous for blind people to cross the street alone or without sighted assistance.

How often do any of us sell ourselves short when we believe that because we are blind we cannot explore a new neighborhood, take a vacation without a sighted person as a companion, apply for a job, or browse in a shopping mall?

Marc and Patricia Maurer and their children, Dianna Marie and David Patrick.

A PURCHASING ALLIANCE

by Marc Maurer

To one extent or another all of us as adults reflect the experience of our childhood. Marc Maurer is President of the National Federation of the Blind. He learned the value of collective action early on. Here is how he tells it:

Twenty dollars was for me a vast sum of money in the 1960s. I knew that it would be years (perhaps decades) before I possessed so much. The sum was so impossibly great that I never even tried to get it. Then, things changed.

I grew up in a small town in Iowa in the 1950s and '60s. Because I was born blind, I was sent over a hundred miles from home to attend the school for the blind. Most weekends, and during the summer months, I could come home. Otherwise, I lived, ate, played, slept, and attended classes at the school for the blind. By 1963 the Maurer family had grown to include Mom and Dad, five brothers, and one sister. Our family appears in retrospect to be much like the ones you read about in books. Mom baked cookies, bread, and rolls. There was always plenty to eat, and the food was good. In my family all the children had one pair of shoes. They were purchased each fall and were expected to last until the next new pair, purchased the following fall.

Pocket money was not plentiful. We were always thinking up schemes to get it. When I was small a penny was quite spendable, a nickel would get you much of what the candy store had to offer, and a dime would fetch anything on display. If a boy had fifty cents, a thing which happened almost never, much of what was to be found in the toy department at the dime store was within reach. We (my brothers and I) set up a lemonade stand in front of the house, but it didn't generate much income. Most of the potential customers were the other kids in the neighborhood. They didn't have much more money than we did. The lemonade business usually brought us two or three cents. Sometimes we collected as much as a dime, but never more than that.

When I was 10 or 11, my mother taught me to make bread. I was so proud of the results of my first effort that I shared them with a neighbor. My neighbor liked the bread, and offered to buy a loaf. From this developed the weekly baking service. My mother made me a deal. If I would bake bread for the family, I could also bake some for sale. The loaves that I sold sometimes brought in sixty cents a week. Store-bought bread was sell-ing for between nineteen and thirty-six cents a loaf.

Boys in my home town made their money by de-tasseling corn or walking beans in the summer and by shoveling snow in the winter. Because of my blindness, I was not welcome in the agricultural pursuits. However, I did shovel snow. I was always sorry when the snow came on weekdays because I was expected to be at school. There wasn't much time for shoveling before the school bell rang. One of the other kids in my class generally skipped school when the snow fell. On the following day, he would boast about the wallet full of money he had collected the day before. I was sorry not to have the money, but I didn't dare skip school.

The standard for conduct in our family was well established. If a kid wanted to do something out of the ordinary, permission from a parent was required. This did not mean that the parent would provide the means for doing what the kid wanted done. One time my brother asked my mom if he could have a bicycle. She told him he could. He wanted to know where he would get the money to buy it. She explained to him that it was his problem. He could have the bike, but he would have to earn the money to buy it himself.

I learned to swim in the first grade, and I thought it was more fun than almost anything else. I looked forward to swimming lessons with great anticipation and was sorry when they were over. Whenever the pool was available (but this wasn't very often) I could be found in the water.

Of course, school begins in the fall and ends in the spring. The swimming pool at the school for the blind was not available to me during the summer months. The closest publicly-available pool was over a mile from my home. Sometimes I could persuade my brothers to go with me, but sometimes I could not. Besides, swimming in the public pool cost money, and money was not plentiful.

When I was in the fifth or sixth grade, I learned that above-ground swimming pools were made. The biggest one in the Ward's catalog cost a little over twenty dollars. I got the idea of forming a buying syndicate. I didn't have twenty dollars, and I didn't think I could save that much. I persuaded my brothers to help me collect enough cash to buy a jointly-owned swimming pool. It took us months. We employed every means we could think up to bring in money—hunting for empty returnable soda bottles to be turned in at the gas station for two cents apiece, running errands to the post office for the elderly neighbor lady for five cents, raking leaves for twenty-five cents, and especially saving our allowances.

As primary thinker-upper and manager of the alliance, I served as treasurer. Each nickel and dime that came my way was cherished and hoarded against the day that we would have enough to place the order. In my home town there was no Montgomery Ward's retail establishment. Instead there was a catalog store—a fairly small storefront office with Ward's catalogs, a very limited selection of display items (not for sale), and an ordering desk. We figured the costs to the penny, including postage and shipping. I remember the important day. We trooped into the catalog store and counted the money out on the counter. Our order was duly taken, and we received the official copy, marked "paid in full." We were advised that shipping would take up to four additional weeks. After the months of scrimping and the work to bring the money together, it seemed like an interminable length of time. We went home to wait.

Every day we checked with Mom to see if she thought the package would come. Finally, a postcard arrived telling us that the box had been delivered to the catalog store and could be picked up at our convenience. We thought that the best thing would be to go get the carton right away. We fetched it home on a coaster wagon and opened it in the back yard. The pool consisted of an outer cage or frame to give the assembled parts their shape, a large plastic sheet shaped to fit into the outer cage and serve as the body of the pool, and fasteners to keep the liner in place. There was also a complicated set of instructions, that not even my father could understand. Nevertheless, we got the whole thing set up and filled it with water.

Swimming in the pool was fun, but I think working and saving to get it were a major part of the reason I liked it so much. Combining resources and working together with others made it possible to accomplish what would otherwise have been out of reach. At the end of the 1960s I joined the National Federation of the Blind. This organization which brings together tens of thousands of blind people from all over the United States changed forever the possibilities for accomplishment and progress in my life. The blind of America were working together and combining resources to achieve what would otherwise have been beyond our reach. We needed more than twenty dollars; we needed the encouragement of our blind brothers and sisters and the strength which comes from working together. I did not know that blind people could be farmers or chemists or electrical engineers or physicists or mostly anything else. Then, when I joined the National Federation of the Blind, things changed.

I learned that I was not limited by my blindness to idle hours and unfulfilling tasks. Instead, with the help of others, I could study at the university, enter a profession, and contribute to my community. It was even better than getting a swimming pool.

THEY DIDN'T WANT ME TO GO TO SCHOOL

by Darrell Shandrow

Darrell Shandrow is a junior in high school. His mother Betty is President of the Parents of Blind Children Division of the National Federation of the Blind of Arizona. Here is what can happen when parents of blind children get the support and help they need when faced with raising a blind child. Darrell tells it from his point of view:

I have congenital glaucoma. I lost my left eye when I was little, and I have very little usable vision in the other. I was also born deaf, but I have been able to hear since age five.

My parents and the National Federation of the Blind are helping me to live independently. My parents felt that it was important that I learn cane travel and other orientation skills at an early age so that I would be independent. By doing so I have been able to participate in public service events and communicate using amateur radio for the last four years.

My parents said that I could do anything I set my mind to. I was raised as a normal person who cannot see. I was not over-protected, and this is the major reason I can function normally.

My parents always felt that I should be allowed to function on the same grade level in school as that of the sighted. My mother took classes at the University of Arizona in Grade II Braille, Nemeth Braille Math Code, abacus, structure and function of the eye, and daily living skills.

With this knowledge my mother helped me learn how to read and write and to have a normal life. By tutoring me at home, she made sure that I was not held back.

Due to my experiences with amateur radio, my parents felt that I was ready to use high-technology equipment. They got me an Apple II-E computer, an Echo III speech synthesizer, a printer, a Braille 'n' Speak note taker, and computer software that is written for the blind.

This technology makes things go much easier in school. I can take notes on the Braille 'n' Speak at school, and when I get home, I can send the notes to the computer, where they are printed and saved onto a disk.

The National Federation of the Blind has reinforced my independence. I can't help but get that feeling of independence when I'm around the blind adults I know in the Federation. I feel that the National Federation of the Blind promotes independence in many ways. I feel that one of the major ways is through the national convention. It's great to be around so many independent blind people.

My family and I had to fight for me to be allowed to attend public school, and the National Federation of the Blind helped us do it and paid the legal costs. We won, and I am now a junior in high school and have a 4.0 grade point average.

There is a saying on the masthead of the *Braille Monitor*, and it's what makes us special: "The National Federation of the Blind is not an organization speaking for the blind—it is the blind speaking for themselves," and that's it for me.

LADIES AND GENTLEMEN OF THE JURY

by Peggy Pinder

At the time Peggy Pinder made the following remarks at a convention of the National Federation of the Blind she was an assistant county attorney in Sioux City, Iowa. Today she has her own private law practice in Grinnell, Iowa, where she has served on the city council and is otherwise active in political and community affairs. She has reduced her blindness to nothing more than a minor annoyance, but it was not always like that. When I first knew her, she was lacking in self-confidence and agonizing over what she might be and become. Like countless others in the National Federation of the Blind she has drawn strength from and found role models in the organization—and also like countless others, she has given (and continues to give) strength and encouragement in her turn and to serve as a model for others. Here is how she tells of her work as a county prosecutor.

"Good morning, ladies and gentlemen of the jury. As the judge has already told you, my name is Peggy Pinder, and I represent the State of Iowa in this case. As you have already noticed, I am blind."

These are the first words that I speak to every panel of potential jurors that a defense attorney and I are questioning before we select those twelve persons who will render a verdict in the criminal prosecution at trial. My employer, Woodbury County Attorney Patrick C. McCormick, is an elected official with the power to hire, supervise, and fire assistants, whose positions have been authorized by the county board of supervisors.

Nine other assistant county attorneys and I occupy the entire third floor of a beautiful and historic courthouse in Sioux City, Iowa. We handle criminal prosecutions and other statutory duties under the Code of Iowa for a county of about one hundred thousand persons in extreme northwest Iowa—where the states of Iowa, Nebraska, and South Dakota meet. I have held this position for over four years.

I love the work that I do. I like working closely with my colleagues, and I enjoy a good argument with the defense attorney in a jury trial that is a hard-fought and a well-fought case on both sides. I am regularly astonished, distressed, and uplifted by the things that people will do to each other and to themselves. There are always variety and novelty in a prosecutor's office.

I begin each morning by walking into the police station, threading my way amongst the citizens who are present to plead guilty or not guilty at nine o'clock arraignments, and amongst the citizens who are present trying to bond an arrested relative out of jail. I walk into my office and pick up the phone.

I have often startled an early visitor by singing out cheerfully into the phone, "Who's in jail today?" I check the jail to be sure that everybody arrested since office hours the day before will be charged or released by noon. I also pick up all the drunk driving charges from the night before, which must be filled out and presented to a judge to whom I swear that the information thus displayed is true and correct.

I then begin to interview the witnesses for morning trial. This is the first time that I have met my morning witnesses or have heard of the facts of the individual cases.

What I have just described is the first half hour of my job, and it can get pretty hectic. The other attorney assigned to the police station and I then go into court and begin trials of simple misdemeanors to which the defendants have chosen to plead not guilty or which the State of Iowa (that is me) is not willing to plea bargain. Simple misdemeanor cases are primarily tried by a judge rather than by a jury, and the judge begins the case by saying, "Miss Pinder, call your first witness."

I stand up and say, "The State would call Trooper Swanson," and then begin to try the particular case. Simple misdemeanors include, in Iowa, most traffic offenses; simple assault cases where injury is not very grave; thefts under fifty dollars, which usually are shoplifting cases; public intoxication; and other assorted minor violations.

I do believe that I have heard most of the excuses people have for doing what it is that they do. There was the man who told the judge that the reason he was speeding at ninety-five miles per hour in a fifty-five mile per hour zone was because a bee had gotten between his right leg and the drive shaft, and that he was trying to crush the bee against the drive shaft before the bee stung him—during which he inadvertently floored the accelerator.

During cross examination I asked the defendant if he had told this rather remarkable tale to the state trooper, and he said, well, no, he hadn't done that. The gentleman was found guilty.

I prosecuted a blind man once. It was for smashing out a windshield of a neighbor's car with a hammer, then running off down the street—but not quickly enough to avoid being seen and identified by the neighbor, who pressed charges.

The blind defendant was sworn in and walked up to the witness stand, which has one step up along the way. The blind defendant was not carrying a white cane or using a dog guide. The defendant tripped on the step. His lawyer then mentioned this tripping and asked if there was a reason why the defendant had tripped.

This blind defendant then replied that he was blind and stated under oath that he had not smashed the windshield and, moreover, could not have done so. He could not have been the culprit because, after all, he was blind, and therefore could not run away.

Well, I'm a patient person, and I waited until this blind defendant's wife got onto the witness stand. She testified, and the blind defendant's wife and I had ourselves quite a discussion about the normality and competence and the ability of her blind husband, the defendant. The verdict was guilty.

We never know what will happen in a police station. When conservation officers—persons who enforce Iowa's Fish and Game laws—bring violations of the fishing laws into court for trial, they invariably show up with the actual fish (carefully frozen and tagged) to wave in front of the judge's face.

And last month in a courtroom filled with police officers and other persons waiting to testify, we had an assault. The relatives of a victim, so incensed at the simple seeing of the defendant, jumped him in the back of the courtroom and beat him unconscious.

When simple misdemeanors are over for the morning and everyone in jail is either charged or has been released on my signature, stating that the person will be charged later, I then return to the courthouse and begin working on the more serious misdemeanor charges.

More serious misdemeanor charges come into the office in the form of police reports, which I must review on a daily basis. I review all the reports submitted to determine if the facts there recounted constitute a crime and, if so, which specific offense. If the facts do constitute an offense, the correct charge is then specified and recorded as "charge approved." If no offense is alleged, or if more work must be done on the case, the charge is denied; and the reasons for the denial are recorded.

I never know what may be sitting on my desk when I get back. One time I had a cat murder in which a five-year-old girl saw a man—she had no idea who the man was—drive by in a car and simply blow her pet cat to bits with a large hand gun. There was the case of the good neighbor, who simply gave shelter to a nearby resident when her boyfriend started to beat her unmercifully. Now, this good neighbor (in turn) was felled by a blow from a tire iron for his pains by the irate boyfriend.

Once a case is approved, the case is assigned to one of the attorneys in the office for all further handling. The next step in handling is preparation of the actual criminal charge. This involves choosing the precise language by which the defendant will be charged and writing the minutes of testimony.

The minutes are full and fair statement—this is what the Iowa law says—of the testimony which each witness will give, and other evidence to be presented by the state against the defendant. This requires that I go through the reports and prepare a full and fair statement of each witness's minutes.

The minutes are required by Iowa law to inform the defendant of the precise nature and circumstances of the charges brought against him or her, and they also serve for prosecutors as a kind of mandatory preparation technique. We must think through the case as though we were trying it before it is even filed, and write out a summary of the evidence that will be given against the witness.

In the years that I have been employed at the county attorney's office, the misdemeanor caseload has doubled each year; and the staff has stayed exactly the same size. How do I write all those minutes? Well, circumstances have forced me to find more and more efficient ways of doing the things that I must do under the law.

Today, I file an average of two to three charges a day. When there is a case in which the defendant will not plead guilty and about which I feel so strongly that I think there must be a trial, I go to court. I begin every jury trial by reading to the jury the exact criminal charge.

After I read the charge, the other attorney and I present our case to the jury, and then a conviction or dismissal occurs. In addition to trying cases, I also do a number of other functions in the Woodbury County Attorney's office including the handling of extraditions, the teaching of police officers how to do their jobs better, and (I think this is the most important thing of all) changing what it means to be blind.

I live in a community of eighty thousand, and I know that the fact that I am a blind lawyer has changed people's attitudes in Sioux City about blindness. Someone comes into my office. They want my help, and they don't really care whether I'm blind or not. Someone comes into the courtroom and sits across the defense table from me. They don't care whether I'm blind or not. They just wish I wasn't as effective an attorney as I am.

The most important thing of all, though, is that whatever I do in my job, I have found ways of doing it. People often ask me how I can do this or that given task, and usually I have answers. And the reason I can find an answer is because of what I have gained from the National Federation of the Blind and especially from Dr. Jernigan. I have the confidence in myself to know that I can walk into that courtroom and find a way of convicting that defendant. It doesn't matter whether I can see or not. The truth isn't discovered by whether you can see or not. Dr. Jernigan was the first person in this world who ever showed confidence and trust in me; and, I hope that I have lived up to his expectations.

SIGHT UNSEEN

by Dr. Elizabeth Browne

Dr. Elizabeth Browne is a college professor who happens to be blind. Here she tells an unusual story. When her story is no longer unusual, we in the National Federation of the Blind will have gone a long way toward finishing our work.

"To be or not to be." That is indeed the question. Whether to note one's blindness in writing when applying for employment or not has troubled many people with various disabilities for far too long. This dilemma has, pardon the expression, dogged me for many years. As I have searched for teaching positions in various local colleges and universities, my practice has always been to let the quality of my credentials speak for me.

But last year something remarkable occurred when I found myself once more searching for openings in local colleges and universities. I began by flooding the market with resumes and letters of inquiry and following up with endless phone calls to countless local colleges and universities. The summer wore on, and I was wearing out.

As the fall semester drew near, I had determined to resign myself to the obvious fact that all positions were full and I should set about completing an extra degree I had been working on for a long time.

The week before classes were to begin, I received a phone call from the chair of the English department at Mundelein College, and she said, "I have your resume in front of me and just happened to notice how well-suited you are for our particular department's needs."

I listened, thinking sarcastic thoughts to myself, "Of course I am!" I muttered to myself. "It's about time somebody noticed." The summer search had been long, and interviews apparently fruitless.

Well, with many apologies for the short notice, the voice offered me a couple of classes, starting in five days. "Will you come aboard? We'd sure like to have you with us." But I had decided to complete yet another degree to make me more academically desirable than ever, so that, when I was turned down somewhere by someone again, they might at least pause and consider what they were losing.

I said, "I'm not interested. I have decided to forego the joy of part-time teaching for this term." Then it happened. "You'd be doing me a big favor, and I wouldn't forget it. Please say yes. You'd like our department, and the college is really a great place to work."

After several phone calls and deep soul-searching, I agreed, and then the following incredible thing happened. "I haven't time to interview you properly because of all the last-minute details, so I'll meet you after your first class next week, and we can have a cup of coffee together, get to know each other a little. Your contract, office key, and library card will be at the front desk. Just pop in and pick them up, and everyone will be saying, "Hi" to you because I told them you were coming. I knew you would accept." And she hung up.

I was stunned. I remember a book, Take Charge, which advised job seekers not to surprise a prospective employer by not telling him or her that you are blind. That's a bad start. I returned to the phone and tried to track her down in order to insist on an interview.

"Why?" she said, "I already know you from reading your excellent credentials. We'll have coffee after your first class when I will have a little time to chat about this and that." And again she hung up.

I agreed with her. My qualifications, my credentials are good. These are the basic reasons to hire someone for a job. But I could not forget that advice about not surprising your potential employer or, in my case, chair of the department. Once more I phoned, trying to break the news to her.

"Would it be okay if I dropped in and walked about the campus, getting used to it, so my dog, guide dog (I emphasized the word dog), would be accustomed to it? Would that be all right?" I had pictures of chairpersons hiding behind their secretaries, whispering that they were gone for the day, when I surprised them in their offices, and I was trying to avoid the chaos.

"I just want my guide dog—like Seeing Eye dog—to get used to the building," I said; and she calmly responded, "Oh, you have a dog. Won't that be wonderful to have a dog on campus. I'll be so glad to meet both of you after your first class. See you on Tuesday." So, I retrieved the contract, signed it, wandered about meeting very friendly people, and then set about to get at least a few chapters of the texts taped.

Tuesday, after a long morning class, I emerged into the hallway outside my room and found the chair of the department waiting for me so we could have coffee together. "How was your first class? By the way, the dog is lovely. Welcome to both of you."

This is the way it should be. When one is prepared, qualified, capable, there should be no taint of stereotyping or prejudice. For the first time I had been hired sight unseen. I had dreamed of this miracle often, and now I have lived to tell the tale.

Postscript: Mundelein College has just been affiliated with its much larger neighbor, Loyola University, and I again set forth hoping the next department chair will display similar traits.

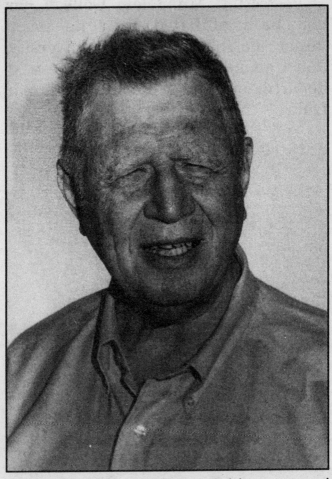

Abraham Nemeth is a world renowned mathematician. He is, incidentally, also blind.

TO LIGHT A CANDLE WITH MATHEMATICS

by Abraham Nemeth

Mathematics is a field which has often been considered beyond the capacity of the blind to master. This attitude continues to exist despite the evidence presented by the careers of world-class blind mathematicians such as Dr. Abraham Nemeth. In 1985 Dr. Nemeth retired, having spent forty years teaching college-level mathematics. His successful career has provided inspiration and hope to later generations of blind students interested in pursuing jobs involving mathematics.

In fact he invented the basic system for reading and writing mathematical and scientific materials in Braille which has been used by thousands of blind students. Here Dr. Nemeth tells the story of his struggle—first to obtain

*an education in mathematics and then
to obtain a position teaching it.*

I was born congenitally blind, on
the Lower East Side of Manhattan in
New York City. And I want you to
know that my parents raised me in a
very close and loving family. I had a
brother and a sister and two sets of
grandparents and lots of aunts and
uncles and cousins. We led a very
happy life. And although my parents
were both immigrants and lacking in
any kind of formal education, they in-
stinctively knew not to over-protect
me on account of my blindness. So I
became street-wise in a tough neighborhood on the Lower East Side of
Manhattan at a very early age.

Without knowing it, my father
taught me what today would be called
mobility and orientation. Whenever
we walked to a familiar destination,
he would take me there by a different
route. As we talked, he would tell me

such things as "We are now walking west, and in a moment we will be making a left turn, and then we will be walking south. We are passing a luncheonette, and after that we will be passing a bakery. Now the traffic on this street is one way going west. On the next street the traffic is one way going east, and there is a fire hydrant at the corner. Across the street there is a mailbox." So he instilled in me a very good sense of direction.

He also taught me the formation of printed letters by letting me touch the raised letters on mailboxes and on police and fire call boxes. He bought me wooden blocks with raised printed letters to play with, and he got me large rubber stamps on which I could feel the printed letters.

My elementary education began at Public School 110. Now you know that New York is such a big city that we run out of eminent people's names, so we just put numbers to the schools.

The one I went to was Public School 110, which happened to be within walking distance of my home. One of my aunts walked with me every day to and from school.

In my daily activity, I attended regular classrooms with all the sighted students for general curriculum subjects like arithmetic, spelling, and reading. But when the sighted students were engaged in activities like art, penmanship, and things of that kind, I returned to the resource room for training in specific blindness skills like Braille, typing, and even geography. There was a very large globe of the world with raised land masses and even more highly raised mountain ranges. Because of family circumstances, I went to live and continue my education at the New York Jewish Guild for the Blind in Yonkers, New York.

At the Yonkers Home children were encouraged (although not required) to engage in activities like music, hand-crafts, light sports and athletics, and religious education after school. While I was there, my father came to visit me almost every Sunday, no matter how severe the weather was. My mother would come whenever her busy household chores would allow— about every other week, I would say. They would bring me my favorite foods, and they were refrigerated and dispensed to me during the week by kindly kitchen staff.

In the spring and summer months many of my uncles and aunts would also come to visit me. We would all go to a picnic area in a nearby park and enjoy the food they brought as well as such activity as the park provided. My father's favorite was rowing.

One of my grandfathers was partic-ularly attentive to me, and he gave me the religious training that I now pos-sess. He would try to find messages that would be encouraging to me and that would serve as a guide for me as a blind person. One of those messages, which has stayed with me and which has had particular impact on me during all the years that I was growing up and by which I am still guided, is: "It is better to light a candle than to curse the dark."

Now you may not believe this, but at school I experienced particular difficulty with arithmetic. I graduated from the eighth grade of PS 16 deficient in mathematics, but with my father's earnest and sincere promise to the school that he would see to it that the situation was remedied.

So I enrolled in the fall at Evanderchild's High School in the Bronx, to which I was also bussed back and forth from the Yonkers Home. In one year's time, I not only caught up with all the arithmetic skills I should have had in elementary school, but I also received top grades in a first-year algebra course in which I was enrolled.

I continued to do well in all my high school courses, and during this period I became keenly aware of an ambition to be a teacher—particularly, believe it or not, to teach mathematics. One of the boys at the Yonkers Home was a good friend, but he was one grade behind me in school. As I learned algebra, I shared with him my knowledge and my enthusiasm on that subject. When he entered high school a year later, he was able to pass an algebra exam with honors and was thus exempted from first-year algebra.

In due course I graduated from high school and returned to live at home with my parents and my brother and my sister, who by now had moved to Brownsville, Brooklyn.

Then it was time for me to go to college. By that time I had already acquired independent travel skills. I knew the routes of all the New York

City subways and most of the Brooklyn bus lines. Equipped with this skill and with a high proficiency in Braille, I entered Brooklyn College.

I knew that I wanted to major in mathematics, but my guidance counselors were not at all supportive of this goal. They insisted that mathematics was too technical a subject for a blind person, that notation was specialized, that there was no material available in Braille, that volunteer or even paid readers would be difficult to recruit, and that no employer would be likely to consider a blind person for a position related to mathematics.

Counselor after counselor told this to me. You know, my wife told me that her mother said if three people tell you that you are drunk, you better lie down. So after several counselors told me this, I obediently declared psychology to be my major—a subject more amenable to the abilities of blind people, my counselors told me.

I took as many psychology courses as I could fit into my schedule. Nevertheless, whenever there was an opening for an elective course, I always chose one from the math department. In taking these courses, there were two things that I did which were, I would say, decisive in my later career. When I found that there was no way of putting mathematical notation down in Braille, just as my counselors warned me, I began to improvise Braille symbols and methods which were both effective for my needs and consistent from one course to the next. So this was the beginning of the Nemeth Code.

The other important skill I developed was the ability to write both on paper and on the blackboard. Sometimes it was the only method I had of communicating with my math professors. And although I was certainly no calligrapher, my handwriting was perfectly adequate for these purposes, and it was surely far superior to the alternative of shouting and arm waving.

In this way I graduated from Brooklyn College in 1940 with a B.A. degree and a major in psychology. Nevertheless, I succeeded in having completed courses in analytic geometry, differential and integral calculus, some modern geometry courses, and even a course in statistics.

I knew that a B.A. degree in psychology was not a sufficient credential for anyone intending to enter that field professionally. So accordingly, I applied for graduate admission to Columbia University. My grades were adequate to ensure my acceptance at that prestigious institution, so in 1942 I graduated from Columbia University with an M.A. degree in psychology.

Meanwhile, it was time to begin looking for a job. The only work I could find was of an unskilled nature. At one time I worked at a sewing machine, where I did seaming and hemming on pillowcases at piece-work rates.

I worked for seven years at an agency for the blind, and there I counted needles for Talking Book phonograph records. I collated Talking Book records. I loaded and unloaded trucks in the shipping department. I typed letters in Braille to deaf-blind clients of the agency, transcribing incoming Braille letters from these and other clients on the typewriter. I also designed and organized itineraries in Braille so that they could be read by Helen Keller.

After graduating from Columbia University with a master's degree in hand, I began to look earnestly for work more suited to my training. The employment environment for the blind is never too hospitable, as you well know. But in those days, it was more inhospitable than it is today. In 1944 I was already married; and as time went on, my wife perceived my growing frustration.

After working all day at the agency, I would find relaxation in taking an evening course in mathematics. By 1946 I had already taken all the undergraduate math courses offered by Brooklyn College, and my wife perceived that I was much happier in mathematics than in psychology. So one day she asked me if I wouldn't rather be an unemployed mathematician than an unemployed psychologist.

Well, I began to wonder how we would support ourselves if I quit my job and went to school full-time, working toward a graduate degree in mathematics. My wife suggested that I give up my job and do just that. She would go to work while I went to school. If I couldn't find work as a mathematician even after completing my training, I could always get an unskilled job like the one I was currently holding at that same skill level, she pointed out.

By 1946 the war was over. Men were returning to civilian life. At Brooklyn College there was a large contingent of men who had taken a first-semester course in calculus, and now (a war later) they were returning to enroll for a second semester course in calculus. I leave it to your imagination how much of the first semester they remembered.

So I offered to be one of the volunteers in a corps that was organized to assist those men. I offered to be one of their volunteers after classes were over in the evening. Each student was stationed at one panel of a blackboard which ran clear around the room. Each wrote on the board as much of the problem as he could do, and the volunteers circulated helping the students to complete their work.

I would ask the student to read me the problem from his textbook and then read as much of the solution as he was able to put on the blackboard.

Many times the blackboard panel was blank. I would do my best to show the student how to proceed.

Unknown to me, I was being observed by the chairman of the math department. One Friday night I received a telegram from him. He informed me that one of his regular faculty members had taken ill and would be disabled for the remainder of the semester. He asked me to report on the following Monday evening to assume that professor's teaching load.

Over the weekend I got the textbooks, boned up to know just enough to teach the following Monday evening, and launched my teaching career.

My ability to write on the blackboard, I believe, was the difference between continuing as a mathematics teacher and finding some other work to do. I continued this way, doing part-time teaching at Brooklyn College.

In 1951 I again applied to Columbia University and was admitted as a doctoral student toward the Ph.D. degree in Mathematics. My wife went to work.

In the summer of 1953 I registered with an employment agency for teachers. I received a call from that agency to report to Manhattan College the following Monday, there to conduct a course in the mathematics of finance—a course I had neither taken nor known anything about. But anyway, I made sure I knew what to do.

Manhattan College is a school run by the Christian Brothers. Brother Alfred was a little dubious when a blind man showed up, but he really had no choice. Classes began in an hour. However, when the summer course was over, Brother Alfred naturally assumed that I would return to teach in the fall, and he handed me my teaching schedule for the semester, beginning in September.

When January came, I received another call—this time from Manhattanville College to fill in for a professor who was on sabbatical. Now Manhattanville College is a very elite girls' school run by the Order of the Sacred Heart. As a matter of fact, Jacqueline Kennedy attended that school, although not in the time that I was there.

Dean Mother Brady received a glowing letter of reference from Brother Alfred, and so I had no difficulty securing the position at Manhattanville College. Commuting to Manhattanville College was an entirely different matter, however.

To do that commuting, I had to walk six blocks from home to the local BMT subway station, take the train to Fourteenth Street in Manhattan, and change at Fourteenth Street from the BMT to the IRT line through an intricate maze of stairs and tunnels which, however, I was already familiar with.

Then I had to take the IRT to Grand Central Station. I had to negotiate a complicated route through the New York Central Railroad, and that took me to White Plains, New York, where finally I was picked up by the school bus for the final fifteen-minute ride to the school in Purchase, New York. And of course I had to do this in reverse at the end of the day.

The Sunday before reporting to work, I went alone to Grand Central Station; and there, all day long, I practiced negotiating the route between the IRT subway station at 42nd street and the Grand Central Railroad Station. The most important landmark on that route was the New York Central Railroad Station Information Booth. Every morning I would stop at that booth and inquire on what track the 8:02 for White Plains would be leaving. It was a two-hour commute each day, and I was surely glad when the semester ended.

It was time to begin to search for permanent employment. By 1954 I was becoming tired of part-time work. The search for employment is stressful for anyone, particularly for a blind person. So I embarked on a campaign of letter-writing with a view to securing permanent employment.

I consulted hundreds of college and university catalogs in the local library to determine which ones offered a math curriculum in which my teaching skills would be valuable. I arranged my choices in the order of geographical preference—by section of the country.

I composed a master letter, tailoring it from time to time as circumstances dictated, and I sent out about 250 letters and resumes. I felt it necessary to inform a potential employer in advance about my blindness.

Most replies were negative. They went something like: "At present we have no opening for a person with your training and experience." Many of them were noncommittal: "Thank you for inquiring about a position at our institution. We will keep your letter on file and will contact you if any opening should materialize in the future." Sound familiar?

Some were downright hostile: "We do not feel that a person with a visual impairment can effectively discharge the duties required of professors at our institution."

Nevertheless, I did receive two letters inviting me to appear for an interview: one from the University of Detroit and one from the university in Boulder, Colorado. Since, however, the University of Detroit offered a position leading to eventual permanence and tenure, I responded positively to the invitation from that institution first.

My wife and I both appeared at the university's request. I was interviewed for a full day, and at the end of the interview we were told to return home and that we would be informed of the outcome within a week. So I mentioned in passing that we were going on to Boulder, Colorado, for another interview.

The University of Detroit is a Jesuit university. The following day, early in the morning, I received a call from Father Dwier. He told me that the position was mine if I wanted it. He was calling early so that I could cancel the trip to Colorado if I so desired. I accepted on the spot.

I went to work at the University of Detroit as an instructor in 1955. And in due course I progressed through the ranks to become an assistant professor, an associate professor, and finally a full professor. Along the way I was awarded tenure, and I also completed the requirements for the Ph.D. degree in mathematics and got it from Wayne State University. I received that degree in 1964.

For fifteen years I taught all kinds of courses in mathematics at the University of Detroit. But it was becoming increasingly evident to me that my training and skills would soon become obsolete unless I acquired knowledge and skill in computer science.

Accordingly, I applied for, and was fortunate to receive, a grant from the National Science Foundation to spend two summers at Pennsylvania State University in State College to train in computer science.

Each session was nine weeks long, and all the students in this program were also college teachers. The pace of instruction was, to say the least, quite lively. My wife and I gave up the comfort of a nice home in Detroit to live in a dorm room for nine weeks of a hot summer during two consecutive years. These were 1968 and 1969.

When I returned to the University of Detroit in the fall of 1969, I designed and implemented a graduate curriculum in computer science, and I taught most of the courses. They included elementary courses like FOR-TRAN and ALGOL and more advanced courses like data structures, artificial intelligence, non-arithmetic programming, automation theory, systems programming, and so on.

During my early years of studying and teaching mathematics I realized that no adequate system existed to represent complex mathematical concepts in Braille. So I set about inventing my own system. Eventually it became a very efficient tool. It worked well for me, and others who learned about it asked me to teach it to them. In 1952 my system was published as the Nemeth Code for Braille Mathematics.

The Nemeth Code features very close simulation of the printed text, and it is that feature which has made it possible for me to communicate with my students just as if I were holding the printed text in my hand. Very complicated formulas I put on cards which I arranged in a small card file in my left jacket pocket in the order in which I planned to present them. At the right moment, I casually walked up to the board and put my left hand into my pocket, read the formula from the top card, and copied it with my right hand onto the blackboard. It gave the students the impression of what a big genius I was, and I tried not to disillusion them.

I have been retired ever since September of 1985. I tell my friends that looking back on my working days, I reflect that work wasn't that hard. But it took a whole day.

I believe that the experience that I have had in my lifetime demonstrates how important are the early acquisitions of Braille skills, facility in mobility, a knowledge of print practice, and good attitudes. Equipped with these skills, a blind person can progress as far as his motivation, his ingenuity, and his talent will permit. Without them, a blind person is restricted to semi-literacy and lack of independence.

SUPREMACY

by Lois Wencil

Both guide dog and cane users would probably agree that life is more lively and complex with a dog. Canes don't look intelligent, cute, or patient. No one is tempted to pat them or talk to them, and while one's children may occasionally experiment with the cane, a toy lawn mower or baton can usually be substituted with great success. In short, there isn't much competition for the affections of or the control over a white cane. Moreover, despite the attractions of devotion and companionship, guide dog users must go outdoors in unpleasant weather and work constantly to maintain in the dog's mind and that of every human being in contact with the team that the blind person is in command and controls every situation. Sometimes this is easier to accomplish than others. Clearly, how-

*ever, committed guide dog users find
these annoyances a small price to pay
for the satisfaction of working with a
responsive animal. Here Lois Wencil of
Millburn, New Jersey, gives us an
amusing look at this ongoing struggle.*

From the time our son arrived
home from the hospital, friends would
ask me if I wasn't afraid that my guide
dog was jealous or might hurt the
baby. As he grew, it was, however,
Steve who terrorized her and
stretched her endless patience. When
he crawled, who better to chase? How
still she remained as he pulled himself
up by her fur. She seemed to know
that if she moved he would fall. Fawn
did learn to jump that spring; on several occasions she gracefully cleared
the gate that confined Steve to our
first floor. His attempts to cut his
teeth on her resulted only in mouth-
fuls of hair. Although we tried our best
to rescue her and barricade her from

him, she felt compelled to be near me;
I needed to be close to him. She, therefore, learned to tolerate this invader
into what had once been her domain.

First a front pack, then a backpack,
and finally a stroller pulled behind
kept him safe and her out of his reach
when we were outdoors. Sitting pret-
tily at my side, she watched carefully
all who stopped to admire our carry-
about. My pats and praise were what
she wanted.

As he became too heavy and pride-
ful to be conveyed, she slowed her
pace to accommodate his stride. Paus-
ing at the down curb, I would scoop
him up and carry him across the
street. Our purchases were carried in
a camping backpack now; my purse
was left at home; I wore only clothes
with plenty of pocket space for tissues,
lollipops, and money.

All went smoothly until we began
discussing crossing streets; red light
means..., green light means...,etc. We

learned to be quiet at corners so Mommy could hear the traffic; he learned stop, look, and listen before you cross the street. He took great pride and joy in knowing when we could safely cross. Then Steve began to command in his deepest, strongest voice, "Forward, Fawn!"

What a quandary; learn but don't practice! If she should respond, should I correct her? Yes! We discussed and rediscussed this point of order, but he was so very proud of his new knowledge. "I'll tell the dog, Mom! My job." In this case, however, there could be no opportunity to let him try.

So we struggled on. He now was growing heavier; at four he would not be treated like a baby. A second traveler would be on board in about five more months. The pregnancy made carrying him both imprudent and dangerous.

In total frustration he began to demand, "Leave dog home; I'll wear the harness!" This was out of the question. "Don't use a cane like Daddy; I'll take you. I'm your big helper." I quickly put a stop to his even trying on the harness because Fawn did resent it. The result was a tug of war between them. The struggle for supremacy raged on!

On a windy spring day we all began a trip for a light load of groceries. "Go, Mommy! We can cross."

With trees swishing, it was difficult for me to hear. "Please be quiet so we can listen."

"No! Go! Forward, bad girl."

Dropping my harness, I patted my friend. "Good girl!" Then turning to him, "Do not tell the dog what to do. I give the command, and she moves when it is safe."

This was too much for the budding child-traffic guard to bear. Enraged, he sank to the sidewalk and began to screech. Enough was enough for poor Fawn too. She lowered herself to the pavement and, uncharacteristically, began to whine. What a sight to behold! First I got one up into position and then turned to the other. In the meantime, the first had gone down once again. A car stopped so its owner could offer assistance. However, when I offered both my charges to him as a gift, he beat a hasty retreat. Spanking time had arrived. We drank water instead of juice that afternoon. A week of playing only in the yard convinced Steve that Mommy alone gave the dog commands. For some time after that episode, he remained at home with Dad or a neighbor while the dog and I went shopping.

Supremacy had been determined. When my daughter eventually took her place as a toddler walking beside me, she also learned to cross streets with less talk and more action. Yet today we all still travel safely.

National Federation of the Blind
You can help us spread the word...

...about our Braille Readers Are Leaders contest for blind schoolchildren, a project which encourages blind children to achieve literacy through Braille.

...about our scholarships for deserving blind college students.

...about Job Opportunities for the Blind, a program that matches capable blind people with employers who need their skills.

...about where to turn for accurate information about blindness and the abilities of the blind.

Most importantly, you can help us by sharing what you've learned about blindness in these pages with your family and friends. If you know anyone who needs assistance with the problems of blindness, please write:

Marc Maurer, President
1800 Johnson Street, Suite 300
Baltimore, Maryland 21230-4998
Your contribution is tax-deductible.